Robt O'Sullivan Day

November 3, 2024
Escondido Arts Partnership Gallery,
Escondido, California

Inspirations Gallery
San Diego Writers, INK
Liberty Station, Pt. Loma, California
November 10, 2024

Tributes

Poets INC
Poets Inland North County
262 E. Grand Ave.
Escondido, CA 92025
poetryscenestealers@yahoo.com

©Individual Contributors   All rights reserved

No part of this book may be reproduced, stored in a retrieval system or transmitted by any means without the express written consent of the Publisher.

First published: by Poets INC, through Garden Oak Press, on August 15, 2025

ISBN-13:   979-8-9879532-4-2

The views expressed in this collection of tributes are solely those of the contributors and do not necessarily reflect the views of the Publisher, and the Publisher hereby disclaims any responsibility for them.

Typesitting and Formatting by Garden Oak Press
gardenoakpress.com
gardenoakpress@gmail.com

Opening Remarks, Robt O'Sullivan Day

November 3, 2024

How fitting that on the eve of a Presidential election which many of us worry threatens something sacred, we gather here to celebrate Robert O'Sullivan. He is the best of us.

Robt is not simply part of our community, he builds community. A gardener of poets, he has nourished so many of us, always reaching out. I learned from his lifelong friend, Dixie Elder that this trait of character dates back at least to his teenager years.

From his first arrival in San Diego, kindness and generosity of spirit have been hallmarks of Robt's approach to poetry and life, according to one who shared those days with him, poet Lizzie Wann.

Giants of our regional poetry community have come to the Gallery today to share their love and thanks for Robt. You will hear from Sharon Elise, Michael Klam, Marit Anderson, Jim Moreno, and others. Everyone agrees this celebration is a good idea.

One person made it a reality. She embraced the concept and ran with it, gathering local support, approaching the Mayor's office, notifying all of you by e-mail—even setting up the Gallery for today, ordering the cake, coordinating the potluck snacks, and safekeeping the official proclamation. That person is Gail Eason.

Please be up-standing as we celebrate a hero among us: Robt O'Sullivan.

The document proclaiming today, Sunday, November 3rd, 2024 as Robt O'Sullivan Day will now be presented by his honor, The Mayor of Escondido, Dane White.

— Bill Harding
founder, *SDPA*

to a SRO-crowd of more than 100
at the EAP Gallery, Escondido

Contents

BILL HARDING
    OPENING REMARKS   3
JAY M. MOWER
    Catalyst   9
LESLIE HENDRICKSON-BARAL
    O' Robert   10
    Let us toast our Word-rhyming Hero   10
ANDY PALASCIANO
    Robert,   11
KATHY KEOGH
    Robert O'Sullivan   12
CAROLOS F. TARRAC
    Echoes of Creativity and Kindness   13
JON OHL
    a poets tribute   14
MATTHEW CHRISTIANSCHER
    Doors   15
MARIS PAULE DELOS REYES
    A Testimonial for Robt   16
MARY ANNE TRAUSE
    Dear Robert,   17
DAVID L. RUGELY
    He had a hat   18
CAROL SHAMON
    Meeting   19
JOYCE RUGELY
    For Robt   20
SANDY CARPENTER
    I Stopped. . .   21
KATHERINE PORTER
    Robert   22
ELIZABETH YAHN WILLIAMS
    Autumn 2024   23
NATHAN GRINSHPUN
    What Does One Need?   24
KATHY O'FALLON
    Robert O'Sullivan   25
ROBERT THOMAS LUNDY
    O'Sullivan
    d
    e   26

JAN BEATON
    Oh Sullivan, Oh Sullivan   27
JEFF BETTGER
    Robert O'Sullivan Day   28
LIZZIE WANN
    My dear Robt,   29
ANNETTE FRIEND
    For Robert O'Sullivan   30
BARBARA DEMING
    Congratulations, Robert   31
JIM BABWE
    R.O.Apostrophe.S.S.   32
LINDA MEEKER
    Happy Robert O'Sullivan Day!   34
GAIL EASON
    For Robert O'Sullivan day   36
NANCY FOLEY
    Robert   38
JEAN E. TADDONIO
    Poet Robert   39
DIXIE ELDER
    From the First Day...   40
DANIELLE ZHANG
    Thank You   43
JIM MORENO
    To the Poet of Lights & Sun Shines   44
STEVE MCDONALD
    Dear Robt   47
MARIT ANDERSON
    In Honor of Robert O'Sullivan Day   48
KEN BUHR
    Sunday Afternoon Art Work   50
DEANNA BUHR
    The Forum   50
MARCY LLAMAS SENESE
    Hi Rob   51
MARIA & JOEY DELOS REYES
    Dear Robt   52
JUDY SISSON
    Robert   53
KATHY 'FSW' DERENGOWSKI
    Dear Robt   54

LISA RATNAVIRA
    Thank you   55
TED WASHINGTON
    A GREAT YOUR DAY   55
MARY QUIGLEY
    So happy for you   55
PENNY PERRY
    Tribute to Robt   56
VERONICA ANDERSON-CAIN
    Thank You, Robert   57
KATIE KEMPLE
    Dear Robt   58
MARY O'CONNOR, RSM
    Dear Robt   59
DEBBIE HALL
    Thirteen Ways of Honoring   60
WILLIAM HARRY HARDING
    Trane   64
SHARON ELISE
    A Tribute to Robt O'Sullivan Schlieth   66
BRANDON CESMAT
    To Robt O'Sullivan on His Day   67
MICHAEL KLAM
    The Poetry Host Haiku   68
JUDY REEVES
    Closing Remarks   69

Appendix
    Proclamation: *Robt O'Sullivan Day*   72
    Photographs
        Dane White and Robt   74
        Robt, reading   74
        Sharon Elise   75
        Michael Klam   75
        Jim Moreno   75
        Gail Eason   75
    Fliers
        Robt O'Sullivan Day   76
        Tribute   76

About This Book   77

Robt O'Sullivan Day
November 3, 2024
&
November 10, 2024

Tributes

Catalyst

for Robert

Universe ebbs and flows
began or ever is
no matter or dark
Star Wars or Star Trek
Schroeder's cat lives
or dies—doesn't matter
Living large:
What you make of
what you got
"There is no reality
except in action,"
wrote Sartre.
So the man who cares
for others, dares
to help them shine
lyrically, rhythmically
while honing his craft
with talent given
from the Unknown
flourishes in a life
of significance.
So be it.

LESLIE HENDRICKSON-BARAL

O' Robert

There lives a man of passion
Pay heed and stay alert
He lives in Escondido
Please praise our poet, Robert

This is a man of substance
He's known both far and near
He lives his life with purpose
His rhymed truth always clear

Our publishing Super Hero
He speaks and writes his Truth
A virtue always honored
A Life Lesson learned in Youth

Sallying forth with poise and purpose
Signup sheet including All
At the helm of every meeting
Our Word warrior standing tall

Let us toast our Word-rhyming Hero

Step out of your shoes
Your feet seek to surf your soul
The journey starts here

Robert,

You have been a light to the poetry community in so many ways. You have been a support to so many, myself included.

One poet who you supported really summed up the help you gave to the community: Mel Takahara, a poet who bravely faced the pain of this world.

I remember, after one of your readings, I approached Mel and told him his poems were very moving. And he looked at me like I had punched him in the face. The pain that Mel spoke of in his poems wasn't imagined to evoke a response from an audience, it was real. His intention was not to be a moving poet, but to address pain with bravery, sincerity and love.

Robert, your readings allow a space for real feelings and real breakthroughs to be shared and supported unwaveringly.

I have one of Mel's poetry books, *The Waiting Child*, and on the cover of the book, it has the words NOT FOR RESALE.

Note: Robt O'Sullivan served as Editor of *The Waiting Child* (Garden Oak Press: 2019).

KATHY KEOGH

Robert O'Sullivan

His Irish voice sings
His Irish heart keeping time
His Irish soul soars

CAROLOS F. TARRAC

Echoes of Creativity and Kindness

Among whispers of rhyme and metaphor,
I met you long ago,
as the Monthly Open Mic filled the air
with the beauty of verse.

When I arrived,
you welcomed me,
with warmth that made me feel at home.

A soul of endless creativity,
a guide for poets and artists,
your kindness shines like a quiet flame,
lighting the way for all.

Your poetry—
A melody that moves the soul,
each line alive with life,
each word echoing in the air.

In every verse, your presence endures,
a lasting inspiration
to those you've touched—
A beacon, a friend,
Inspiring us all to write and dream.

a poets tribute

Words flow like the breeze,
words flow like the hurricane,
words flow as truths,
words flow as lies,
words flow as love,
words flow as hate,
words flow as passion,
words flow as despair,
but where are my words?
Poets call out on paper
Their tears and laughter
Now black and white markings on paper
And those feelings released
Out into the world
So that others with feelings
Now have words to express themselves
The poet's words can create culture
And lead exploration
Into the depths of you
The poet poised in his script
has words for every moment
has words for every feeling
as they oscillate inside him
but oh, to know which word
will really express that feeling
any word can be amazing
if it's placed in the right order
with the right syntax
the right emotion
at the right moment
with a hanging pause.

MATTHEW CHRISTIANSCHER

Doors

*Dedicated to Robert O'Sullivan,
someone who opened doors for me and many others.*

everyone's seen them
doors
closed
because
of your
who, what
where or when
keeping your songs
your stories
your truth
in a notebook
on an unknown
dusty shelf
Then there are a special few
Bodhisattvas
for those looking
to sing their songs
tell their stories
or paint their truths
Someone who opens doors
and changes lives.

MARIS PAULE DELOS REYES

A Testimonial for Robt

I met Robt at the Escondido Museum during an art exhibition/poetry reading. The art show attendees and poets were invited to the first Sunday of the month Poets INC poetry reading by him. Robt gives everyone equal access to poetry and spoken words. I am grateful to have met him. He's inviting and makes poetry fun and very accessible. Robt's inclusive personality made me understand and gave me the confidence that my difficulty with the English language is, actually, an asset! Through his encouragement in my writing, poetry and while reciting my poems during our open mics, I became a poet!

Thank you, Robt, for creating a healthy community for us poets, and for your incredible support and mentorship to me and many others. I greatly appreciate your mentorship which also helped to reignite my love for the arts and the expressive arts.

Congratulation Robt for a well-deserved recognition in our community! We celebrate you!

A genuine person
With a love for poetry
Inspiring many

Dear Robert,

I first met you about five years ago when you brought copies of Summation to Marit's Awaken the Poet Within. I was impressed by how friendly you were and how everyone seemed to know you. Then I got to meet you again through *Summation* and Poets Inc. You are such a wonderful welcoming leader in our poetry community in San Diego.

I was especially touched by your coming to Adam Masava's show of Kenyan art at my daughter's preschool and your willingness to consider his work for showing in Escondido. Adam was quite touched by your generosity. And I also loved your offer to hold a kids' reading at the gallery when my grandson's teacher was working with eighth graders on writing poetry.

Thank you so much for being you. I have felt supported by you, as I'm sure many others have, in so many ways. We are lucky to have you as a voice for poets and poetry in San Diego's North County.

With admiration and affection,
                      Mary Anne

David L. Rugely

He had a hat
for Robt

call it amazing, first time I met him
but it was more brotherly
at a time when I did not know
that I was in need of encouraging, he was there indeed
big ole smile,
greetin' like, sayin'
I should write
a writer? No not me...
at times I dream of that, naw not me
He reminded me of Paris, and he said I could be a writer...
with that laid-back Pigalle vibe
you know Pigalle is electic and smooth and bumpin'
lots of jazz from the bistros thru
the air and everyone
just chillin', for the heck of it,
and likin' it, him too
I can even say lovin' it
by the way they all strolled
on that pre-autumn night
bistros so inviting and inviting all to a
pinot or chardonnay and the likes
Left bank-ish, know what I mean? people be like
Like, they born to chill, just chillin' and you know, that hat
He had a hat...
smilin' real chill 'neath his hat, my brother Rockin' that hat
He had a hat...

Meeting

Meeting Robert O'Sullivan felt like one of those wonderful synchronistic, meant to be moments that can change the direction of one's life. I'd always loved poetry but ceased calling myself a poet for 35 years while I had my children and concentrated on my career. I was finally going to retire in 2022. That winter, my friend Diane, invited me to a Poetry Slam at the La Paloma theater in Encinitas. I hadn't been to a slam in years and decided to attend. During the intermission, a nice man took the stage and talked about a poetry event he held in Escondido once a month.

The next evening my partner was showing his handmade wood furniture at the EAP gallery in Escondido. There I saw that very same nice man who I had seen on stage the evening before. I introduced myself and he asked if I wrote poetry. I told him I used to. He told me about a publication he produces every year called *Summation*. He had a few empty spots that needed poems. I submitted to *Summation* and began attending Robert's once a month Poets Inc gathering.

I've noticed that there are two types of artists. One type is competitive and protective, the other type is gracious and welcoming. Robert O'Sullivan epitomizes this second type. He is one of the most gracious and encouraging people I've ever met. He has provided me and so many others a safe and nurturing place to share our deepest thoughts, fears and dreams. Robert's commitment to poetry and inclusiveness is a rare jewel that we all benefit from. I'm happy and honored to be celebrating him on his much-deserved proclaimed day.

JOYCE RUGELY

For Robt

When I think of our dear Robt, I am lost in his eyes.
These eyes show a lovely sensitivity, a joy, a pain
Which have made him the wise, loving, caring,
Beautiful, inclusive soul that he is.
He has always been a strength, encouragement,
Inspiration to me, personally, and in my writing life.
It is only fitting that we celebrate Robt
For all he is, and for all that he continues to do and be for
Each of us and our thriving community of
Talented artists and lovers of written and spoken words.
With my love, admiration and deep appreciation.

I Stopped. . .

I stopped writing poetry when my friends started
dying as some of my friends wrote greater about mortality
and their own impending illness then their upcoming
Death. Some wrote angrily about their invisibility
and created a testimony in which we can learn
what it is like to walk the avenues of American towns
as a ghost. Some wrote poems to memorialize loves,
or to embarrass politicians or arts funding agencies.
But I just counted 82 folks I knew with Covid, was fond
of most of them yet turned on suffering and death then
in poetry. Is it poems or is it me? The era? I believe
if Shelley or Milton or Tennyson could do it, it means
something. Why should I think their ages made death
any more manageable a subject than mine? But....
whenever I sat down to try, I stopped in despair.
Whatever the political advantages of slogans
of the time, it wasn't the right words I looked for
but some way to make silence heard in lines
of verse, and I never found it. Now even that sounds
like a device to me, like special pleading. No, let
someone else do it. So I stopped writing poetry
but I still loved a stanza. All that other smart stuff--
tropes, the caesura, enjambment--I can live without.
But the STANZA---wow! Still, I stopped writing poems
when the internet replaced the phone. A writer
destroyed the sonnet by inviting his beloved to
"just pick up the phone and call him sometime"
thus no more need to plead and seduce through verse,
now we all plead and seduce in lower case
as only the freest verse used to be. Then along came
ROBERT almost 20 years ago, and instead of giving up
the writing of poetry I ran toward it and asked myself,
" Would it really be so terrible if I wrote just one more line?"

Robert,

this is how important your work is to me and the world. Meeting you and being greeted with such warmth and generosity of spirit is very rare. The importance of hearing and writing poetry in my life, and the transformative power in the overall world health cannot be overstated. Life is complex and too often painful, and yet poets continue to produce beauty through words and images that feed our hearts and minds. Arriving in the gallery to hear and share poetry brings a breath of fresh air-- a setting aside of life's woes, we join others to hear voices barely known, yet we become almost instantly connected-- this amazing journey is the miracle of poetic rhythm and phrase. Robert, you have created a community where I feel grateful to belong. I hope to not miss as many months next year. Thank you Robert for all you do!

      Love and hugs to you,
                    Kate

ELIZABETH YAHN WILLIAMS

Autumn 2024

Rex and King
of poetic things
by composite writings,
'tis he who reigns as Host first Sundays,
though wordsmiths weekdays to edit and credit.

A Salutation for Rob't,
aka Robert O'Sullivan Schleith,
from an EAP and Poets INC Member

NATHAN GRINSHPUN

What Does One Need?

What does one need?
A little love,
A little compassion,
Once in a while a little passion...
Freedom to create and share with a friend
A cake, a roast, a poem, a house...
Keep under the armpit a little gray mouse,
A mouse that loves you like no one before,
Like no one will love you any time anymore...
You can talk to her,
She is a friend...
Talk about anything,
Talk to no end...
The ones on the right
And the ones on the left,
Trust those
Who want all of us dead...
But forget about the mice,
All I truly want is again
Save
Peoples
Lives.

Robert O'Sullivan

Steady as a redwood,
Clever as a crow,
Funny as a mongoose,
Generous as the sun,
An ever-ready bunny,
Talent in every toe.

Rob't O'Sullivan's example of leadership reminds us that putting the ego aside and committing to the work of community makes all things possible. He is poetry in action, evoking a transformative experience, in this case, through fellowship.

I am deeply grateful to have such an example in my life. As well, his poetry reflects true dedication to the art in its excellence. Thank you, Rob't.

O'Sullivan
d
e

Three cheers for Bob O'Sullivan
The laureate of slam, bar none!
Each month he gives all bards a voice
Whatever their stylistic choice.
We owe him much—our creditor
Is also our best editor.
Thanks to his work, *Summation* lives
And to us, endless pleasure gives.
Although the lighting's sometimes dim
The pickings here are never slim.
He'll always pull the very best
Works from the monthly special guest.
No diamond in the rough is he
He sparkles effervescently
A jewel like the Cullinan
Is Robert (Schleith) O'Sullivan!

JAN BEATON

Oh Sullivan, Oh Sullivan

Oh Sullivan, Oh Sullivan! For where art thou Oh Sullivan?
Well, thou cannot possibly be sleeping. A busy man tis he.
The monthly poet readings do limit the times he has been able to say,
"Good night, goodnight poeting is such sweet sorrow that I shall say
good night 'til it be morrow." Oh Sullivan, Oh Sullivan the *Summation*
Anthology editing is calling. It's a task too much for an O'Neill, a
Yeats, a Wilder, a Joyce, but not for the king of "Slam Poetry." Robert
the fifth is on the throne.
But words are whispered from the balcony " Uneasy is the head that
wears a crown." That's not right, nothing in Oh Sullivan's head is
easy. And who is the Chairman of the Board? It is surely not old Blue
Eyes. It is our own poet of swoon. If that is not enough each Tuesday
he pulls up his overalls, grabs his raggedy straw hat, throws his pitch
fork over his shoulder and calls for his taxi. "Well, a horse, a horse,
his kingdom for a horse of the course." Now mounted he rides
through each Middlesex, village, and town on the way to the farmers
market singing like a good Chairman of the Board should, "I did it my way."
His way was the best way, fairest way and most poetic way.
Fondly and thank you so much!

JEFF BETTGER

Robert O'Sullivan Day

Many of the people who know Robert will write about his kind heart. His love of poetry. His amazing memory of poems. His legendary humility. His place in the history of poetry in San Diego County. His leadership role in creating a new *Summation* volume each year. His organizational skills making Poet's Inc. a reality each month.

Because each will be done by others who have known Robert much longer than I have, I want to recount two short stories of how Robert's friendship has impacted my life.

After Robert invited me to a poetry event. I began writing some simple, but heartfelt, poems. Having not written poetry before, I sent a few to Robert for his feedback. His encouragement was a surprise and a blessing to me. I had been struggling to take care of my sick father and needed something happy and positive to balance the sadness and lack of sleep I was experiencing. It was Robert who encouraged me to submit poems to *Summation* and to a local poetry contest. The positive outcome of both changed my life dramatically. The validation I received provided the lift to my spirit that was so very needed. Poetry became the artistic outlet I didn't know I needed. A means of self-therapy. A connection to other kind-hearted people. A rally point for my family.

Second, within that year, my father passed away. After the funeral concluded, Robert asked if I had noticed the poem inscribed in the stained glass in the chapel. I had not. He informed me that it was *Crossing the Bar*, by Lord Alfred Tennyson. When I returned home, I sat quietly and read the poem. I felt a great calmness and thankfulness that I was blessed to have a friend who noticed and recognized that classic poem. I knew that poem was my father waving goodbye to me as he crossed.

Robert O'Sullivan, enjoy this day. Your day. We salute and thank you.

LIZZIE WANN

My dear Robt,

As you know, my memory is complete shit, so I don't remember when we met. Also because it feels like I've always known you, or at least a version of you. I know you had a whole other life before you arrived in San Diego, before you started coming to Java Joe's. That must be it. We met at Java Joe's sometime in the mid to late 90s. You were living in Hillcrest with your beloved, Bob. You published my work in Driftwood Highway, and somewhere along the way, we clicked and my hopes for bringing the poetry slam scene to San Diego were made real because of you. You took on the heaping majority of work to build what would become a thriving, not just slam, but poetry, scene. From the Rendezvous Cafe to Urban Grind, trips to Big Sur, and you doing all the legwork to get PSI certified (when that was a thing!), fundraising, and getting the teams to the destinations. Man, that was ALL YOU. And not to mention, that you, in your own right, are a fantastic poet and performer! I was happy to be a witness. I was happier to be in community with you. I was happiest to be your friend, going on, what 30 years now?!?!? How can that be? I'm not sure how I would have gotten through all these years without you. You've been a shoulder to cry on, a pillar of integrity and grace, a generous supporter of poetry newbies and veterans, and always, my dear friend. I am so thrilled for you to be receiving this amazing proclamation to solidify your immense contributions to poetry and to the San Diego poetry community. May you and your talents live long.

love,
Lizzie

ANNETTE FRIEND

For Robert O'Sullivan

R—Rites Ribald and Racy poems and stories that make us laugh out loud with his Raucous characters

O—Observant and Open to all kinds of poetry and people and incredibly Organized!

B—Bolsters poets' confidence by his warmth and welcoming everyone to Poets INC for readings

E—Effervescent and Energetic – How does he accomplish all he accomplishes???

R—Radiates a joy and love for poetry and art that have created an amazing community

T—Tender and kind to newbie poets, oldster poets, and everyone in-between

Dear Robert,

With gratitude and thankfulness for the wonderful community you have created Robert over the years, and all the hard work you put in throughout the year to keep this community thriving and growing. Also, for all the personal kindnesses you have shown to me through your encouragement and kindness.

You are so appreciated for all that you do!

        Love,
               Annette

Congratulations, Robert

Congratulations, Robert! If anyone is worthy of being recognized, it is you, dear friend. I don't remember how many years ago I was invited to check Poets INC out, but I was caught up immediately in the wonder of your poetry group. I do remember being there for the stapled copies of Summations though. You, Robert, have been my inspiration, my mentor, always so helpful, and so generous with your encouragement. I miss being a part of your scene, seeing all of the wonderful poets you have drawn in; I will return one day.

Celebrating you, Robert, with love and appreciation.

R.O.Apostrophe.S.S.

Understated Uniter.
Poetry Promoter.
Word Warrior.
Verbal Vaquero.
Metaphor Manager.
Simile Sayer.
Figurative Fighter.
Literal Leader.
Courageous Communicator.

Don't call him Ishmael.
Melville might mind.

Call him Robert.
Add a title from the list above.
Add more than one.

Or add an accurate anecdotal title of your choice.

I know someone who thinks
of Robert as a spy
of some sort.

On the other hand (or leg),
we're talking about an individual
who doesn't sneak around.

Maybe he's an un-clandestine spy--
one who goes about his work
in a way which challenges
the common definition of spy.

On the other hand (or leg),
we're talking about an individual
who blatantly provides many
with opportunities
to be heard.

Do what you like.
Say what you will.

But add the following three words
as descriptors or designators
or metaphorical medals
to describe the mettle of the man.

Gracious.
Generous.
Good.

And these are probably
not enough.

Can I get a witness?

I know I can.

LINDA MEEKER

Happy Robert O'Sullivan Day!

I have had the pleasure of knowing Robert O'Sullivan Schleith through the Summation Art and Poetry Project since 2014. Ten years ago, I was an artist showing my work in the *Summation* Art Exhibit. I was thrilled to discover that poets would be writing to the art in the show. I asked the gallery director, Chrisanne Moats, if I could submit a poem. She said, yes, and I got busy writing. My poem was accepted and I have been participating in the *Summation* Project ever since.

Before I entered my poem in Summation VII, I had been writing pieces of poems in my artist sketchbook, starting with my years in college at Santa Cruz. I have always loved poetry, and sometimes wrote poems for family members on special occasions. The opportunity to write and be published in the Summation Art and Poetry Project was a game changer for me. All of the experiences, observations, and thoughts that had been in my head and jotted down in my sketchbook, finally found a place were they could be shared and expressed with the art community.

Working with Robt has been wonderful. Robt responds to emails within minutes, usually with a clever and insightful comment. Robt has always been encouraging and kind. He was able to get me to read my poems out loud to the group, after years of patient nudging. Robt has a gentle way of coaxing out the talent in all of us. A message from Robt brought me from Covid lockdown isolation, back to writing, at a time when I was yearning to reconnect with people in the art world. The following year, when I was lost in a summer of Long Covid doldrums, a simple note from Robt got me off the couch and creating again. Participating in the Summation Project has been empowering and healing.

Robt knows the artists and the poets and their stories and fosters a warm community of creators. He brings together old and young, experienced and novice, and finds the gems that might otherwise be hidden. The *Summation* Anthology is filled with an eclectic collection of styles and original ideas, a credit to Robt who welcomes and appreciates a variety of art. Robt inspires artists and writers to express themselves in their own voice, in their own way. It's amazing how diverse the poetry is for each work of art in the book. The publication parties are fun and spirited celebrations, whether at Twiggs Coffeehouse, Leucadia Pizza, or the Escondido Arts Partnership Gallery. Robt sprinkles a bit of his own thought provoking poetry in the *Summation* book, a sweet treat, and sometimes Stoner Boomer makes an appearance.

The merging of art and poetry is magic. Thank you, Robert O'Sullivan Schleith, for the opportunity you give to so many artists and poets to collaborate and share their creative work.

GAIL EASON

For Robert O'Sullivan day

Life is an interesting experience, we all can certainly attest to that, right!

Traveling through the years we often meet remarkably interesting people, some more fascinating than others, and there are the weird ones as well.

Lots of stories of interesting people, we all have them, all different in many ways. They cross our path, hang around in your life for a while, leave a memory or two. We all have had that, I am sure.

Then there is the extraordinary person, the one that stumbles into your life unexpectedly. The person that arrived at the right time for all the right reasons. The extraordinary person who you feel a deeper kinship with, a different sort of friendship, a friendship between two people who already know the rules, the way to relate to one another and you know you can count on this one person to always be there. And you trust this one person with your deepest secrets, never spoken before.
That is Robert O'Sullivan, my deepest closest friend. He is extraordinary, he is that person that rarely appears in some people's lives, he is exceptional and fascinating, smart, funny, trustworthy, leaps and bounds above the other folks I have had an opportunity to know over the years. I cannot find a word that describes how this friendship between us came to be, so quickly, but it was meant to be, in the stars, all things aligned. It feels as if it has been a lifetime friendship but has been only for about 3 years. That is Robert O'Sullivan, the man I call my closet friend and never want to be to far away from incase he needs me for anything. I will be there.

Of course, we all know that he's an exceptional writer, poet and MC of Poets Inc. Robert has a long history in San Diego's poetry community but I'm fortunate to see him as so much more than those accolades that everyone will say about him: I am better for having him in my life as my friend and I hope I make a difference in his life in some small way. Thank you, Robert, for being the person you truly are.

So, I leave you with this short poem:

> Why not be that person who lives with full moons in each eye,
> Never turns away from you
> Answers your call, no matter the time of day
> That is always saying – with that sweet moon language
> what others are dying to hear.
> "I speak your language—I hear you—
> I will not go away—I am your Friend."

Robert

Year after year he has been the face of the poetry
   community
supporting the newbies and encouraging the oldies.
People are drawn to his engaging manner,
his attention to detail, his welcoming smile.
Like a well-worn house, he has survived the force of wind
and rain, but has always remained true to himself,
comfortable in his skin. Today we salute you, I salute you.
May you continue to bless us with your presence.

Jean E. Taddonio

Poet Robert

His words carry us
a dolphin tumbling in flight
jubilant success

DIXIE ELDER

From the First Day. . .

Day One, Fall quarter, freshman year 1971 at Northern Virginia Community College (where Dr. Jill Biden is now a professor.) I attended Drawing I and Introduction to World History; rooms filled with fiercely competitive students. All of NOVA's students worked part-time or fulltime jobs, saving money for four year university tuition.

Caught in a panic attack, my German I textbook clutched as a shield against my chest, I couldn't read the print-out of classroom assignments in my shaking hand.

A voice from just behind my right shoulder, "You've got the same book." He held up *German for Begin*ners. "Are you trying to find the right room?"

The boy had large blue eyes and the kindest expression I'd seen on that terrifying first day of school.

"Yes, I'm freaking out."

"This is it." He opened the door for me. A gentleman in this day and age where *anything goes*. That was Robert O'Sullivan. We began talking that moment and haven't stopped since!

He sat in a desk next to mine. On the blackboard were these words, *Frau Eckhart*, along with *Wilkommen im Deutschunterricht*.

It was all Greek to me, although I knew *Wilkommen* from the musical *Cabaret*, which my high school performed in my senior year. Too scared to try out, I was an enthusiastic audience member because my friend, a gay boy called Drac', played The MC.

On week two of German class, Frau Eckart called on Robert and me to read a dialogue and translate the words into English. We carried our textbooks to the front of the room and began:

"Wer ist im deiser Klasse?" (Who is in this class?) I read.

"Alle unsere Freunde" (All our friends), Robert answered

"Wir kennen uns." (We—uh— know us.) I stuttered.

Robert looked at the professor and repeated, "We know us?"

We ran into the hallway, possessed by uncontrollable laughter. From that day on, all either of us had to do to make the other shriek with hilarity, was to say, "Wir kennen uns."

Why am I telling you a story about a German class in the early 70s?

Because WE KNOW US is the definition of Robert O'Sullivan's life.

Robert knows and understands sensitive people.

He cares deeply how those with different brains feel.

Robert knows and encourages poets.

Robert has met and cared about people from all walks of life: elderly, students, people who've come to America from all over the world, and those who have never left the neighborhoods where they were born.

He is close with folks from the GLBTQ+ community. He's friendly with those who are wealthy, middle-class, and people barely hanging onto small homes in poverty stricken neighborhoods.

Robert has worked with folk singers, classical flautists, and theater geeks. He sat with my father—a jazz fiend—grooving to Chet Baker's trumpet. He gave me Sun Ra's *Omniverse* album on my 26th birthday. I danced to that music, filled with divine madness

Robert knows insecure beginning writers. He helps transform words like grit-filled clay into Brancusian sculptures worthy of publication in top literary journals. Robert O'Sullivan can pore through a stack of artworks and pluck out those imbued with magic.

Robert has edited numerous anthologies, and organized art gallery events. He insists that shy poets stand and deliver their words before audiences. Music infuses his voice. And merriment is never far from his heart. [. . .]

When I met Robert O'Sullivan on that first day of German class at our community college, he was an 18-year-old boy eager to begin his adult Hejira. Robert became a true leader. Wherever he lived, from the DC area, then the Shenandoah Valley where he studied at Madison College, was an inspiration. As a singer/songwriter, Robert O'Sullivan toured America, playing guitar and singing in nightclubs, at festivals, and campgrounds until he reached LA. Later, as a citizen in San Diego, Robert founded Slam Poetry events. In Escondido, he's active in the POETS, INC community. He was responsible for ensuring that the City Council continued to fund the Escondido Arts Partnership.

Robert O'Sullivan inspires people to transform their spots in this oft' dark world into a kinder, brighter place.

DANIELLE ZHANG

Thank you so much for helping me finding my passion in poetry writing. Your legacy is not only being an accomplished gifted poet, but to go beyond to pave the way for many of others who may not know that they have an inner voice to be written in poetry form.

我敬你：诗人，诗長，诗友。以诗會友，友情長存！

DANIELLE ZHANG + Art & Culture

JIM MORENO

To the Poet of Lights & Sun Shines:
Robt O'Sullivan-Schleith

It is my nature to be reckless, exhibitionist,
  abandoning, prophetic, cruelly honest.
But to prserve my flesh & sanity,
  thereby lengthening my timeline.
We are the scribes, the historians,
  the exorcists—exalted in ancient cultures,
barely noticed in the modern age. We predict
  the future as we record the past.
We have lived a million lives at once,
  a million times or more.

  Robert O'Sullivan Schleith
  Heart For Darkness

My Dear Robert, this poem has to be a letter,
a way of honoring you for all you've done
for poetry, all you've done for our poetry
community, all you've done for each poet
in this room, all the poets who have flocked
to 262 E. Grand Ave. to perch on poetry
here in this artful nest.

My letter acknowledges how you walked
your talk, lived your walk. You are the
two-spirited man who wrote these lines...

but most of all remember,
should you discover you are lost,
I can help you find your way.. see,
I can double as a compass or a map.

You tripled as a life light, a poetry light,
an inspirational Muse Light.
I watched you talk to young poets
in this room and other rooms lining their
poetry path with lights of encouragement,
lights of nurturing, and yes, lights of inspiration.

And you did the same with me, the
fledgling performance poet, back in
the 90's, you were a light modeling how
to read what inspires me, write what inspires me.
If I'm not inspired by what I read, If I'm not feeling
what I write then my readers, my listeners, will not
feel inspired you see. All this you taught us, not with so
many words, but with the power of your example.

We knew you had Neruda in your heart & soul
when you wrote as the voice for the voiceless,
you penned the poem that spoke for a murdered
black teen whose life was stolen by a white
cop who feigned protect and serve while taking
the teen boy's life. You wrote these lines:

1964 in NYC, just out of sight of the 12-story
World's Fair Unisphere,
a 15-yr-old black child name of James Powell
was shot & killed in front of his 9th-grade friends
by this off-duty white police lieutenant,
sets off six consecutive nights of riots, 500 arrests in
Harlem &more to follow out in Philadelphia, in
Rochester & in Paterson just three short years
before the flowers & the smoke of the Summer of Love;
no John the Journeyman wasn't California dreaming
hadn't moved into Jeannette Macdonald's Bel Air
mansion yet. . .to me, not even 12,
the world was only just now waking up.

And now, we're mostly all elders. just now waking up to
your legacy of leadership here as we listen to your
Song For A Life that is, and was, your song of stanzas
and stories and soliloquies, your series of lights,
spoken reflections as poet, performer, and decades of
light as promoter and organizer for literary arts in San
Diego, as well as the original San Diego Poetry Slam.

[. . .]

You captained San Diego's first team of poets to the National Poetry Slam, and you host Poets, INC (Inland North County) and The Escondido Arts Partnership Literary Series, and so many more.

So this poem-letter is a thank you for the labor of love that you modeled for us all these years.

You *are* our Compass & our Map. . .

I end my letter with acknowledging that we all,
    everyone of us,
have no regrets about you. As a matter of fact,
    we all love you very much.
And there's nothing, absolutely nothing,
    you can do about it. Aho!

        four days before the 2024 Presidential Election

STEVE MCDONALD

Dear Robt,

I just want to take a moment to tell you how grateful I am for all the love and commitment you have shown to San Diego poets and their poetry for so many years. People like you are so important to the world of poetry. Because of you and your work through the Escondido Arts Partnership and Poets INC and so many other poetry venues, San Diego poets have had opportunities to share their work and to meet others who love poetry as much as they do. I still remember how delighted I was when I first attended one of the monthly readings in Escondido. Here was a tribe of poets! And there you were providing a place for them to gather and read and meet other poets. Thank you so much, Robt! You are loved and appreciated by many, many poets in San Diego.

MARIT ANDERSON

In Honor of Robert O'Sullivan Day

I'm down to the wire and the deadline is you, Legs. I've been keeping juicy secrets, just like you poetry tricksters did while planning Marit Anderson Day (July 25, 2023). November 3, 2024 is proclaimed to be Robert O'Sullivan Day – What can I possibly say? How about some juicy secrets never shared about the first time ever I saw your face and Legs—written in February, 2015:

    The host, Robert O'Sullivan, was wearing board shorts; his bare calves were well-toned and hairless. Maybe he was a biker, or a speed swimmer who wants to skim through water like a trout. He looked a little nervous, but didn't seem like an asshole. I liked him – wondered what dark and light shadows have crossed this guy's horizon. How does he mix the paint he splatters on the audience? It's warm and running down my cheek. Feels a bit yellow, with a hint of aubergine and pencil lead.

    I was wearing a cut-off jean skirt, black tights, black t-shirt, black leather jacket, and a black beret. But, I still had the hooters, and would write that poem a few weeks later. I didn't read at my first Poets INC gathering; I listened and soaked in the gallery vibe. Legs mentioned the next month's theme and suggested prompts, which I joyfully turned into a rant about swallows returning to the Capistranos, a mafia family. Yes. He was already running through my veins, giving me permission to do whatever the hell I wanted to do – as long as it was authentic. He loved me way more than I loved me. And I still didn't know if he was a biker, a swimmer, or a shiny trout who'd be tricked by my shimmer; but I had a glimmer—of a teacher and I wanted to be his pet.

Dude, I wrote those words almost a decade ago! This shelter dog found a forever home with you Legs, and we're not done rocking the North County poetry and art scene. Thank you for your patient, loving leadership, and wicked word slinging. You lift me up and, yes I'll get corny—light up my life. Keep showing up and shining!

  Love & Pantsuits,
  Marit ~ *Awaken the Poet Within*

P.S.: I call myself Robert's secret phony Russian girlfriend, but that's not an official title either!

Ken Buhr
Sunday Afternoon Art Work

The steel thread extending
　　　from the gallery's wall
held firmly a sculpture
　　　suspended in space,
performed its role perfectly,
　　　invisible but when seen
strong and reliable.

We stepped to the microphone
　　　in the gallery, before our peers
shy or confident, poems in hand,
　　　for you were there, Robert,
ours the spotlight, you, the steel thread
　　　supporting us,
you, the maestro, leading the band
　　　with twinkling baton.

Deanna Buhr
The Forum

　I love the forum you have made possible for poets,
on poetry. Thank you for that recognition, and
understanding the importance of poets in all our lives.

MARCY LLAMAS SENESE

Hi Rob,

I'm sorry I wasn't able to make it for the celebration of all you've done for poets and poetry in our area.

Nonetheless, I was so happy to know that you were being honored! I will be forever grateful for the encouragement you gave me, and the many opportunities to read my work. I know you have done the same for many of us!!

    My best always

Maria & Joey Delos Reyes

...*calls to you like the wild geese, harsh and exciting—
over and over announcing your place / in the family of
things.*
—Mary Oliver: *Wild Geese*

Dear Robt,

Congratulations on this milestone :) Wow! A whole day in honor of your contribution to the community, such a well-deserved achievement! Today we celebrate you. And thank you!

Robert

Thank you for all that you do and everything that you bring.

Among your many talents you inspire poets with a gentle cohesiveness that gifts us with enthusiasm & a desire to excel.

My life has been enhanced by the poetry events in unexpected ways! Thank you!

KATHY DERENGOWSKI

Dear Robt,

This recognition is well deserved & long overdue. It has been *our* great privilege to know you and call you mentor & friend.

With all love & respect,
Kathy (and of course Casey)

LISA RATNAVIRA

Thank you for all you do for our poetry community and for your kindness.
        Love and friendship,
               Lis

TED WASHINGTON

Have a great *Your Day!*, Robert O'Sullivan!

MARY QUIGLEY

So happy for you.
        Love & blessings,
            Mary

PENNY PERRY

Tribute to Robt

A wonderful poet himself, Robt O'Sullivan Schleith has hosted Poets INC at the Escondido Art Gallery for 20 years. Always welcoming to newcomers and poetry regulars, the gallery is a haven, a place to be heard. Under Robert's gentle guidance poets who have never read in public before feel safe to take a risk.

The audience Robt creates is attentive and encouraging to all. One older poet said that some of us who are no longer able to protest in the streets can come to the gallery and express our outrage about what is happening in our country.

Robt often treats us to his wonderful, lyrical and sometimes funny poems. He frequently features well-known poets from all over the country. Poets sell their books at the gallery.

My family met Robt in 2001. He hosted a reading in a cozy cafe in San Diego. My daughter, then a senior in high school, read a poem, *Pretty*, and the audience clapped so vigorously that the café walls seemed to shake.

When we heard that Robt had moved near our own valley and would be hosting at the Escondido gallery, we were excited. And expectant.

For me, no matter how despondent I might get about the times we live in and our country, when I see Robt and he smiles, I find my seat in the gallery, and know— I'm home.

Thank You, Robert

    Just thought I would compose a quick note to a master of *the written word*. I want to tell you how much I admire you and your work. Quiet, deliberate, thoughtfull, kind—you are a man to be admired and listened to. I enjoyed working with you, and hearing about you (thanks to Gail!).
    You do so much! It's not just that you inspire and encourage: it's boots-on-the-ground, gets the job done, Poet who gives light to all of us.

KATIE KEMPLE

Dear Robt,

Thank you for creating such a warm and welcoming community for Poets INC & the Escondido Arts Partnership. Attending these monthly readings, meeting other poets and having the opportunity to share my work has given me a sense of connection and purpose. That is all thanks to you! You really see and hear people. Your encouragement has kept many of us going, and coming back for more. Thank you!

MARY O'CONNOR, RSM
Dear Robt,

I was never at such a love-fest! And you deserved it all, and more. The little I know of you marks you forever in my mind as the most dedicated promoter of the arts, and more importantly, of people. Your kindness and encouragement has meant a lot to me, kept me going when I felt I was past it. You just seem to pour yourself into things—wonderfully, admirably.

I will never forget you. . .even in Dun Laoghaire.

from Ireland,
after reassignment from Pacific Beach

DEBBIE HALL

Thirteen Ways of Honoring Robt O'Sullivan Schleith

The poet is the priest of the invisible.
—Wallace Stevens

I
Find the paths he's travelled—
follow his footsteps,
learn from him
as you wander
the artist's way.
Remember to breathe deeply,
carefully attend to the world
around you.

II
Listen to
the roots of musicality
in the chords
of his voice
when he performs his verse
& that of others—
inhale the tones
and let them animate
your own voice.

III
Celebrate poetry
in all its forms—grand
and humble.
Scatter leaflets with random
words (nouns and verbs preferred)
onto city sidewalks—
invite all who wish
to shape them
into lyrical lines
of declaration, lamentation,
incantation.

IV
Elevate others—
lift them onto a platform
made of your open palms.
Raise them up
to a long view of the sky,
to a clear view
of their own
infinite potential.

V
Put your arms around
all forms of art—
painting, sculpture,
rivers of music, streams
of slam, ode, sonnet. Notice
the endless ways in which
words, sounds and visions
shape themselves
and each other.

VI
Always remember
to breathe deeply,
carefully attend to the world
around you. If you see
a blackbird, study it
closely. Know
that it has some
wisdom to impart.

VII
Find a body of water—
lake, river or sea.
Walk there at sunrise.
Gather leaves, feathers
and stones Collect
birdsong, coyote arias,
wind's whistle and rush.
Always, always remember
to breathe deeply.

[. . .]

VIII
If you want to make
a poem, a lyric, a story,
don't wait for the muse
to find you. Instead,
open your front door
and step out with
beginner's mind.

IX
Next, clear the deck
of all pesky expectations.
Walk for a while,
then write, draw
or sing about whatever
comes up for you.
Repeat daily.

X
If you get stuck
in your writing, listen
to music, music
that is unfamiliar to you.
If a blackbird
happens to be around,
listen to its song
or chatter. Transcribe
the sounds into
colors, thoughts
and feelings.

XI
Share your creations
with others.
If you are new at this,
and shy, find a herd
of horses (don't forget
to take carrots)
and recite or show
your work to them.

If they approach,
nod in thanks. If
they nuzzle you,
know that your work
is good.

XII
When you are ready to
read your work to people,
know that Robt
has a safe and welcoming
place for you.
Consider it a holy space,
a space to thrive
in community.
Take a deep breath
and share your carefully
wrought words
like the small blessings
they are.

XIII
Take in the applause
you will inevitably hear
in response to your work,
let it wash over you.
Then, turn your attention
to Robt and give him
hearty thanks
as you and the audience
put your hands together
in a rush of heartfelt
gratitude.

Trane

for Robt

He asks for *A Love Supreme*,
"if Coltrane is in your repertoire."
Man—Trane is in nobody's repertoire.
Tougher than Monk,
whose originals Steve Kowit wanted me to feature
behind his performance of *Solo Monk*.
And it's still up on YouTube
for everybody to hear my mistakes!
These poets are killing me.
Should have told the truth: musically,
I am no longer fit for human consumption.
But it's Robert O'Sullivan Day.
Can't burst his balloon.

Trane, like poetry, is breath.
His masterpiece moves off three notes,
one of them repeated: D, F, D, G—
chanted as "A love supreme."
The intonation and the attack,
that's where it lifts off.
Growing up in the Swing Era,
before he heard Bird, or joined the Navy,
before he morphed into Trane, young John
would have heard, even played,
two big hits from famous bands:
Harlem Nocturne and *Everything Happens to Me*.
I feel their melodic structures echo through
A Love Supreme. Yeah, maybe slip in snippets
of both tunes as a pathway
to his teenage soul.

OK—try the opening movement, *Acceptance*,
the first step to prayer. Coltrane wrote it
three years before he died in 1967. He was
not quite 41 years old.

So—Practice. Lube the sax, break in the reed,
build some wind again.
Breath. Music. Poetry. Prayer.
No net.
Better fly!

    (immediate start of musical performance)

Tenor sax: opening flourish of *Acceptance*, then
    vamp the chant: *a love supreme*, into
    first 8 bars of *Acceptance*, into
    vamp the chant, into
    opening 16 bars of *Harlem Nocturne*, into
    vamp the chant, into
    opening 8 bars of *Everything Happens to Me*, then

Vocal: sing first stanza of *Everything Happens to Me*, into

Tenor sax: vamp the chant, then
    arpeggios descending in minor thirds
    —high D to middle B,
    sustain, until out of wind,
    finishing with only breath leaking past the reed.

        performed November 10, 2024
    Inspirations Gallery, San Diego Writers, Ink,
        Liberty Station, San Diego.

        hosted by JUDY REEVES

SHARON ELISE
A Tribute to Robt O'Sullivan Schlieth

We slammed into each other and stayed
a two-step of mutual admiration,
different and fascinated.
He arrives at the podium holding so much love it leaks
out in a glance, word, gesture.
So much love he held him through it all,
camping and caretaking, loving Bob.
So much more than words, his words draw
landscapes, voice draws us in,
lifted in love, grief and sorrow, joy and wonder.

So many years of Sundays at a gallery in Escondido.
so many times we slammed each other.
So carefully he crafted and polished and published. . .
Our Robt, Oh Sullivan, Schlieth.

BRANDON CESMAT

To Robt O'Sullivan on His Day

Yes, Robt, the Escondido Municipal Gallery
was a toy store, a controversial one because of
its mural of a model train that inspired city council
    debate,
but before that it was Bud's Market,
decades before you hosted poems amongst paintings
    and sculptures.
You're standing about where a checkout line began.
Can you sense ghosts of *The National Enquirer* & candy
    bars,
you know, the impulse items? So much seduction in
    that spot.
Where Jim Moreno is sitting is where the bus boy
    bagged the goods.
Sharon Elise is right about where the cash register cha-
    chinged,
That puts the other poets in that row on the conveyor
    belt.
Seretta is sitting by the canned goods,
all that photosynthesis sealed in cylinders and saved to
    re-enter the cycle
at a later date like certain present poems that arrived
    before their time.
Jim Babwe stands with his back to the produce aisle.
For some reason, no one's near the meat counter.
I've no evidence of any of these apparitions I see,
nothing except this poem, so I have to say,
Robt, I love what you've done with the place.

MICHAEL KLAM
The Poetry Host Haiku
for Robt

The host of the show
has only two jobs. TWO JOBS.
1) Pacing. 2) Snacks.

Closing Remarks, Robt O'Sullivan Day

November 10, 2024

What an honor to host the *San Diego Poetry Annual*'s tribute to Robt O'Sullivan at San Diego Writers, Ink.

A poet and participant in and organizer of the San Diego writing community about as long as I have been involved; we both go back to those early 90s when it seems poetry and poets were everywhere and so was he. What a great pleasure it has always been to see this gentle man with his open heart and ready hug at any and all gatherings where poets and writers gather, and to hear him recite his poetry, which, to my mind, doesn't happen often enough. (More, please)

We could do a *Robt O'Sullivan Day* every day and it still wouldn't adequately pay tribute to a man who has given so much to our community of poetry and poets as Robt. I'm still celebrating!

— Judy Reeves
co-founder, SDWI

Inspirations Gallery, SDWI,
Liberty Station, Pt. Loma

Appendix

Proclamation

Robt O'Sullivan Day
November 3, 2024

Whereas, **ROBT O'SULLIVAN** co-founded the ***San Diego Poetry Slam*** team in 1997, nurturing spoken-word poets and teams representing San Diego County in regional and national competitions, highlighting the quality of poets and the vibrancy of the poetry scene in our area, and

Whereas, he became one of the original Regional Editors of the *San Diego Poetry Annual* in 2008, a position he continues to hold, bringing recognition to the excellence of poets in our region, especially those from North County Inland, a group he helped found, and

Whereas, he has hosted an annual reading every May for the *San Diego Poetry Annual* at the **Escondido Arts Partnership Gallery** since joining the SDPA as a Regional Editor, giving local poets the opportunity to celebrate each other's work, and

Whereas, he shared judging duties for the second annual **Steve Kowit Poetry Prize**, sponsored by the **San Diego Entertainment and Arts Guild**, helping to bring national and international recognition to our region by establishing a premiere prize of $1000 that celebrates excellence and the legacy of the late Steve Kowit, noted poet associated with San Diego, and

Whereas, he has edited and sustained **Summation**, an ekphrastic literary journal that combines art exhibited at the Escondido Arts Partnership Gallery and poems written to those works of art, in an effort to manifest in full-color book form the connection between visual art and poetry, while providing recognition to regional artists in each format, and

Whereas, he has mentored a long list of poets for over a quarter of a century, improving their work and reputations, and editing their poetry for chapbooks and for full-length collections, including ***The Waiting Child*** (Garden Oak Press: 2019) by Escondido poet Mel Takahara, nominated for the San Diego Book Award, thereby elevating the level of poetry in our region and beyond, and

Whereas, he has been a key force in running the **Escondido Certified Farmers' Market**, under the auspices of the **Escondido Arts Partnership**, and

Whereas, he has served the Escondido Arts Partnership over three decades, including as a member of the non-profit's board of directors, helping to make it and its gallery a vital force within our regional arts community, and

Whereas, by his example as a noted poet, dedicated mentor, welcoming host, empathetic editor, and charismatic community leader, beloved by his colleagues, peers, and friends; therefore

It is proclaimed that Sunday, November 3, 2024 be declared **Robt O'Sullivan Day** in the City of Escondido, to be celebrated at the Escondido Arts Partnership Gallery during the afternoon poetry reading and re-celebrated at Liberty Station a week later on Sunday, November 10, 2024, during a special poetry reading co-sponsored by **San Diego Writers, Ink** and the *San Diego Poetry Annual*, where in both locations and on both dates he will be the guest of honor.

In witness thereof, I have hereunto set my hand this day and caused the seal to be affixed hereto.

DANE WHITE
Mayor, City of Escondido

Note: The framed document presented to Robt is an edited version of this final draft, submitted to Mayor White's office for approval.

left to right: **Dane White, Mayor of Escondido, and Robt O'Sullivan**

Robt O'Sulliivan

Sharon Elise

Michael Klam

Jim Moreno

Gail Eason

SAVE THE DATE

ROBERT O'SULLIVAN DAY
PROCLAMATION

NOVEMBER 3, 2024
12:00 – 3:00PM

Escondido Arts Partnership Gallery
262 E. Grand Ave. Escondido

Please join us at **POETS Inc** Sunday to officially deliver from Escondido Major Dan White's Office the "Robert O'Sullivan Day Proclamation." This day is in celebration of and recognition for what Robert has spent years supporting - Poetry and the Spoken Word. OR

You are also invited to submit a written testimonial if you wish

Submit any written work to Gail Eason
gaileason0629@gmail.com
Or
Bill Harding
sdeag1@gmail.com

Please RSVP your intentions to the above contacts. All written testimonials should be received by Oct 15th.

Tribute to ROBT O'SULLIVAN

Sunday, November 10 — 3 to 5 p.m.
Inspirations Gallery
San Diego Writers, Ink
Liberty Station, Point Loma

Robt O'Sullivan Day
+
Final *SDPA* reading of 2024

Judy Reeves: host

2730 Historic Decatur Rd. #204
San Diego 92106

About this book

P oets INC is the sole beneficiary of sales of copies of this tribute, in book form, to commemorate Robt O'Sullivan Day celebrations.

Editorial services were donated by Garden Oak Press.

262 E. Grand Ave.
Escondido, CA 92025
760.480.4101| mail@escondidoarts.org

Gallery Hours:
Tues. 11am - 5pm
Thurs. to Sat. 11am - 4pm

www.ingramcontent.com/pod-product-compliance
Lightning Source LLC
Chambersburg PA
CBHW060216050426
42446CB00013B/3086